TRAVEL WITH THE GREAT EXPLORERS

Explore with

John

Franklin

Cynthia O'Brien

Crabtree Publishing Company
www.crabtreebooks.com

Crabtree Publishing Company
www.crabtreebooks.com

Author: Cynthia O'Brien
Publishing plan research
  and development: Reagan Miller
Managing Editor: Tim Cooke
Designer: Lynne Lennon
Picture Manager: Sophie Mortimer
Design Manager: Keith Davis
Editorial Director: Lindsey Lowe
Editor: Kelly Spence
Proofreader: Crystal Sikkens
Children's Publisher: Anne O'Daly
Production coordinator
  and prepress technician: Tammy McGarr
Print coordinator: Margaret Amy Salter

Produced by Brown Bear Books for
Crabtree Publishing Company

Photographs:
Front Cover: Alamy: Design Pics Inc cr; Getty Images: Popperfoto main; Shutterstock: Eric Isselée br; Thinkstock: Photos.com tr.

Interior: Alamy: Yvette Cardozo 20t; Antiques Navigator: 27bl; Archival Research Catalog: 28-29t; Elisha Kent Kane: 20-21t; Getty Images: Hulton Archive 13t; National Maritime Museum: 16t; National Portrait Gallery: 20b, 28b; Pete Carney: 21br; Polar Sea: 21br; Robert Hunt Library: 4t, 4-5b, 6t, 6b, 10, UNK 11b, The New Yorker 12t, 13b, 14l, 18, 19t, 19bl, 24b, Amelie Romilly 28l, 29b; Shutterstock: 25t, 27br, FloridaStock 23c, Max Lindenthaler 7t, Denis Pepin 25b, Miguel Garcia Saavedra 12b, Valentyn Volkov 15t; Thinkstock: Cory Glencross 24t, Eric Isselée 11t, istock 23b, Photodisc 16br, Design Pics 17, Lisa Strachan 5, Digital Vision 7b; U.S. Fish and Wildlife Service: 23t; Westlicht Photography Museum: Susse Frére 14b; Winnipeg Art Gallery: 26.
All other artwork and maps, Brown Bear Books Ltd.

Brown Bear Books has made every attempt to contact the copyright holder. If you have any information please contact licensing@brownbearbooks.co.uk

Library and Archives Canada Cataloguing in Publication

O'Brien, Cynthia (Cynthia J.), author
     Explore with John Franklin / Cynthia O'Brien.

(Travel with the great explorers)
Includes index.
Issued in print and electronic formats.
ISBN 978-0-7787-1703-4 (bound).--
ISBN 978-0-7787-1707-2 (paperback).--
ISBN 978-1-4271-7714-8 (pdf).--ISBN 978-1-4271-7703-2 (html)

     1. Franklin, John, Sir, 1786-1847--Juvenile literature. 2. Northwest Passage--Discovery and exploration--British--Juvenile literature. 3. Canada, Northern--Discovery and exploration--British--Juvenile literature. 4. Explorers--Great Britain--Biography--Juvenile literature. 5. Explorers--Canada--Biography--Juvenile literature. I. Title. II. Series: Travel with the great explorers

FC3961.1.F73O37 2015   j917.1904'1092   C2015-903208-3
                                              C2015-903209-1

Library of Congress Cataloging-in-Publication Data

O'Brien, Cynthia.
 Explore with John Franklin / Cynthia O'Brien.
   pages cm. -- (Travel with the great explorers)
 Includes index.
 ISBN 978-0-7787-1703-4 (reinforced library binding) --
 ISBN 978-0-7787-1707-2 (pbk.) --
 ISBN 978-1-4271-7714-8 (electronic pdf) --
 ISBN 978-1-4271-7703-2 (electronic html)
1. Franklin, John, 1786-1847--Juvenile literature. 2. Arctic Regions--Discovery and exploration--Juvenile literature. 3. Northwest Passage--Juvenile literature. 4. Explorers--Arctic Regions--Biography--Juvenile literature. 5. Explorers--Great Britain--Biography--Juvenile literature. I. Title.

 G660.O37 2016
 917.1904'36092--dc23
                          2015017340

Crabtree Publishing Company

www.crabtreebooks.com   1-800-387-7650

Printed in Canada/082015/BF20150630

Published in Canada
Crabtree Publishing
616 Welland Ave.
St. Catharines, ON
L2M 5V6

Published in the United States
Crabtree Publishing
PMB 59051
350 Fifth Avenue, 59th Floor
New York, New York 10118

Published in the United Kingdom
Crabtree Publishing
Maritime House
Basin Road North, Hove
BN41 1WR

Published in Australia
Crabtree Publishing
3 Charles Street
Coburg North
VIC, 3058

CONTENTS

Meet the Boss

From the 1500s, Europeans tried to find a way to Asia through Canada's Arctic region. They called the route the Northwest Passage. Sir John Franklin made progress in this search, but at a tragic cost.

THE SEA CALLS

+ Young Franklin ignores family advice

+ Trip inspires lifelong passion

John Franklin was born in 1786 in Spilsby, England. At age 14, he joined the navy, against his parents' wishes. Franklin later became a **midshipman** for his uncle, Matthew Flinders. He sailed with Flinders around Australia in 1802–1803. The ship wrecked on a reef, and Franklin spent 51 days stranded on a sandbar before the crew was rescued. Franklin decided he wanted to become an explorer himself.

IN THE NAVY

★ Britain at war

During the 1800s, Britain fought many battles as it expanded its **empire**. Franklin fought at the historic Battle of Trafalgar in 1805, a British victory over a French and Spanish fleet. Franklin also fought in the Battle of New Orleans (right), the last battle of the War of 1812 between Britain and the United States.

TRAVEL UPDATE

Arctic claims lives

★ If you're heading north, take enough food! The British sent Franklin to the Canadian Arctic in 1819 to chart the northern coast. The harsh climate and lack of **provisions** led to disaster. Eleven men died on the expedition. The survivors ate **lichen** and even the leather from their shoes. Franklin earned the nickname, "the man who ate his boots."

In 1836, Franklin became lieutenant governor of Van Dieman's Land, now Tasmania in Australia. In the 1800s, the island was a **penal colony** (below). Franklin believed in educating and treating the prisoners fairly. This attitude won him friends among the settlers, but angered the government. After several difficult years, Franklin was fired. He returned to England in 1843.

Did you know?

Franklin was married twice. He married the poet Eleanor Anne Porden in 1823. They had a daughter, also named Eleanor. The baby's mother died in 1825. Franklin married Jane Griffin in 1828.

My Explorer Journal

★ Franklin was eager to go to sea from a young age. Think why you might want to join the navy. Write a letter to your parents explaining why they should support your decision to join.

Where Are We Heading?

ICE!

Ice stopped Franklin's ships in the fall of 1845, forcing the crew to spend the winter on Beechey Island. Ice trapped them again by King William Island in September 1846.

Franklin's expeditions to the north helped to map new areas of the Arctic lands and seas. His discoveries helped later explorers to navigate through the dangerous Northwest Passage.

OUT IN THE COLD

☛ Arctic proves too much

Franklin first visited the Arctic on a whaling ship in 1818. He led an overland expedition there a year later. During what became a three-year expedition, Franklin traveled the length of the Coppermine River (right). He also explored the Arctic coastline. Supplies ran out and Franklin lost 11 of his 20 men.

RETURN TO THE NORTH

+ Arctic hero furthers exploration

When he returned to the Arctic for a second expedition in 1825, Franklin was better prepared. This allowed him to chart more of the interior and the coastline. Franklin and his party mapped over 900 miles (1,450 km) of coast along the Beaufort Sea.

THE MIGHTY MACKENZIE

★ Beyond the river delta

Almost 40 years before Franklin's second expedition, the Scottish explorer Alexander Mackenzie had mapped a long river that led to the Arctic Ocean. In 1826, Franklin and his men traveled the Mackenzie (left) as well. When they reached the **delta**, the group split in two. Franklin's group headed west toward Alaska while the others journeyed east to the Coppermine River. The successful expedition earned Franklin a **knighthood**.

Did you know?

Before Franklin's last voyage, his wife, Jane, laid a Union Jack flag over his knees to keep him warm. Franklin said, "They lay a flag over a corpse!" Did he have a **premonition** of his fate?

> " Your flag is yet snug in its box and won't be displayed until we get to a more northerly region."
>
> *Sir John Franklin writes to his first wife Eleanor about a flag she had sewn for his expedition*

SPOTTED!

+ Baffin Bay meeting

Franklin's ships sailed into Baffin Bay on his final voyage in 1845. Franklin hoped to keep traveling through Lancaster Sound, north of Baffin Island. The captains of two whaling vessels, the *Enterprise* and *The Prince of Wales*, reported meeting Franklin's ships. Everything seemed well, but the meeting turned out to be the last time anyone saw Franklin and his men alive.

JOHN FRANKLIN'S TRAVELS IN THE ARCTIC

Sir John Franklin's doomed final voyage took him into the heart of what is now Nunavut, in northern Canada. He and his men spent nearly three years trying to find a way out of the Arctic ice.

King William Island

In the winter of 1846, the survivors of the expedition abandoned their ships in the ice northwest of King William Island. They set out to walk across the island, heading south. Artifacts and remains still show their path across the frozen land.

Queen Maud Gulf

In 2014, the wreck of Franklin's ship *Erebus* was found off King William Island. The ship may have moved from where it sank due to tides or the movement of sea ice. The exact location of the wreck is being kept secret to avoid **looting**.

Cornwallis Island

Prince of Wales Island

Peel Sound

Somerset Island

Boothia Peninsula

NORTH AMERICA

King William Island

N

NW

NE

W

E

SW

SE

S

Cornwallis Island
Franklin sailed around Cornwallis Island to try to reach Peel Sound. The way was blocked by ice, so he turned back to make camp on Beechey Island.

Beechey Island
The expedition built their winter camp on Beechey Island. They lived there during the winter of 1845. The graves of three sailors were later discovered here.

Baffin Bay
The last time the ships from the expedition were seen was in northern Baffin Bay. Franklin was planning to sail through Lancaster Sound.

Disko Bay
In summer 1845, Franklin took on his final supplies from the support vessel at Disko Bay, Greenland. The crew also wrote their final letters home.

Devon Island

Lancaster Sound

Baffin Island

Scale 100 miles / 160 km

Key
- - - → Franklin's journey

Locator map

Starvation Bay
This point on the Adelaide Peninsula was the farthest south any of the survivors from the expedition reached.

Meet the Crew

Franklin was a respected naval officer at the time of his final journey. Most of his officers and crew, however, were unknown. Their disastrous journey made them famous.

A LOYAL LADY

★ **Explorer's wife sponsors searches**

★ **Arctic exploration gets support**

After Franklin's first wife died in 1825, he married her friend Jane Griffin in 1828. Jane Franklin helped him set up schools in Van Dieman's Land. After Franklin disappeared, his wife organized and paid for search parties. She continued to research the Arctic and travel until her death at age 83 in 1875.

CAPTAINS AT THE HELM

+ **Experience and youth on Arctic mission**

By 1845, Francis Crozier was a naval officer with several Arctic journeys under his belt. He was a clear choice to captain the *Terror*, the second ship on Franklin's last voyage. By contrast, James Fitzjames (right) was a young officer with no Arctic experience. However, he had joined the navy at aged 12 and traveled widely. After Franklin's death in 1847, Fitzjames took command of the *Erebus*.

WILD CREW

★ Pets go to sea

In addition to the 129 men onboard, the *Erebus* and *Terror* also carried three animals. The most unusual was Jacko, a monkey, who was a gift from Lady Franklin. As they approached the Arctic, the sailors made Jacko clothes to keep him warm. The other animals were Neptune, a Newfoundland dog, and a cat to hunt for rats.

My Explorer Journal

★ Imagine that you are a young sailor at Disko Bay in 1845. Soon you will be eating tinned supplies. Make a menu of what you would eat for your last proper meal before you leave.

Yum-Yum

No one knows what became of the animals on the ships. If the men were starving, they might have killed and eaten the animals as food!

LAST STOP

- ☛ Unsuitable sailors dismissed
- ☛ Final supplies loaded

In July 1845, Franklin stopped at Disko Bay, Greenland. The crew sent letters home and then loaded supplies. Franklin dismissed four men who seemed unfit for the journey. As it turned out, he saved their lives. The other 129 men, including four cabin boys, would meet their deaths in the freezing Arctic.

I'VE GOT YOUR BACK

+ Officer paints icy landscape

George Back, a naval officer, was with Franklin on his 1819 and 1825 expeditions. He also made his own expeditions to the Arctic. When supplies ran out on the first trip to the Coppermine, Franklin sent Back to find help. Back located some native people who brought food to the Europeans at Fort Enterprise. Back was a talented artist who painted and drew many images from his Arctic travels.

Check Out the Ride

Arctic exploration required sturdy ships that could handle extreme conditions and carry plenty of provisions. HMS *Erebus* and HMS *Terror* carried Franklin and his crew on their fateful journey.

BUILT FOR THE ICE

+ Ships reinforced for Arctic trip

Both the *Erebus* and *Terror* were three-masted **bomb ships**. The *Terror* had been to the Arctic in 1836, and *Erebus* had been to Antarctica. Franklin had the hulls reinforced with iron so the ships could withstand crushing ice. A layer of waterproof cloth was put between the double-layered deck to keep supplies dry.

Did you know?

The name *Erebus* comes from Greek mythology. It represented the darkness of the underworld.

HOME FROM HOME

☞ Sailors keep busy

The sailors had many things onboard to entertain them. Each ship had an organ for playing music. Men who could read had access to 1,700 books on the *Erebus* and 1,200 books on the *Terror*. The libraries held books about Arctic exploration, as well as *Punch* magazine and the new novel by Charles Dickens, *Nicholas Nickleby*.

CABIN FEVER

★ **Hammocks for beds**

★ **Little space available**

Only Franklin had a comfortable cabin onboard ship. Other officers often dined with Franklin in his cabin. Fitzjames and Crozier had cabins, but they were both small and cramped. The ships carried so many supplies (enough for a three-year voyage) that the sailors had to squeeze into the remaining space. Many of the crew slept in **hammocks** hung around the deck or in any space they could find.

Desks

Both ships carried school desks, so that sailors who could not read could take lessons during the long Arctic winters.

GREAT LOCO

☛ **Steam engine technology**

The *Erebus* and *Terror* did not rely on wind power alone. The ships carried supplies of coal to run full-size steam engines taken from locomotives. The engines were adapted to drive the ships' 7-foot-wide (2 m) screw **propellers**. This was the first time propellers had been driven in this way. The propellers could also be pulled into the ship to avoid damage from ice.

Solve It With Science

Say Cheese!

Franklin's expedition was the first to take a camera. Since Franklin, all explorers have taken cameras with them to record their discoveries.

Franklin's last expedition had the benefit of new inventions, such as the camera and canned food, but not even the latest technology could save the doomed mission.

CAUGHT ON CAMERA

☞ **Explorer hopes to capture Arctic images**

☞ **Sits for his portrait**

The Daguerreotype was an early camera that was invented by Louis-Jacques-Mandé Daguerre. It produced a photographic image on a silver-plated sheet of copper. Before they set sail, Franklin (right) and his senior officers had their pictures taken. Then they took the camera onboard so they could record images on their expedition.

DRINK UP!
★ **New system cleans seawater**

Franklin did not worry about having fresh water for his crew. The ship's steam engines ran on fresh water. In order to maintain the supply, the ships had special systems to filter the salt from seawater. This made the water suitable for the engines, and also supplied the crew with drinking water.

BITTER LEMON

★ **Get your Vitamin C here!**

★ **Franklin's precautions fail**

In the mid-1800s, explorers knew about the dangers of **scurvy**. They avoided it by getting lots of Vitamin C. Franklin's ships carried 9,300 pounds (4,218 kg) of lemon juice. Franklin did not realize, however, that Vitamin C loses its strength over time or that the crew would be away for so long. Later evidence showed that scurvy had affected Franklin's crew after all.

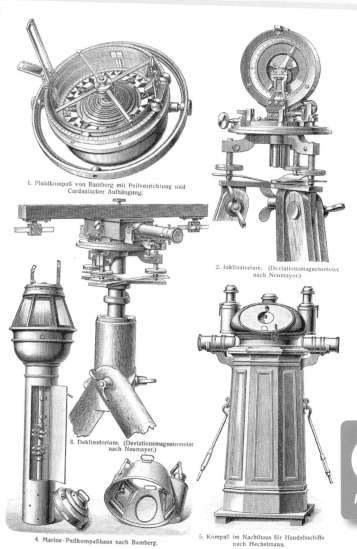

1. Fluidkompaß von Bamberg mit Peilvorrichtung und Cardanischer Aufhängung.

2. Inklinatorium. (Deviationsmagnetometer nach Neumayer.)

3. Deklinatorium. (Deviationsmagnetometer nach Neumayer.)

4. Marine-Peilkompaßhaus nach Bamberg.

5. Kompaß im Nachthaus für Handelsschiffe nach Hechelmann.

MAGNETIC ATTRACTION

+ Explorer to take scientific log

In the 1800s, navigators still did not know about Earth's **magnetic fields**. However, scientists did understand that the Arctic was an ideal place in which to study them. Scientific discovery was an important part of Franklin's Arctic explorations. He wanted to study magnetic declination. This is the angle, or difference, between magnetic north as shown on a compass and true north.

> " Let me now assure you that I am now amply provided with every requisite [need] for my voyage."
> *Franklin writes to his wife from Greenland, 1845*

Hanging at Home

Franklin was an experienced explorer by the time of his final voyage in 1845. He and the people in charge of the Navy took care to make HMS *Erebus* and HMS *Terror* comfortable.

DON'T GO HUNGRY

★ **New technology ideal for sea voyages**

★ **Rush job ruins food**

Franklin's ships carried 8,000 cans of meat, vegetables, and soup, enough to last three years. However, preparation of the food was rushed and many cans were not sealed properly. This may have caused **lead contamination** or spoilage.

DINNER'S READY

☛ **Sailors feast**

A supply ship, *Baretto Junior*, sailed across the Atlantic with the *Erebus* and *Terror*. The three ships stopped at Greenland to transfer cargo. The *Baretto Junior* carried ten live oxen that were killed and eaten. This would have been the last fresh meat Franklin and his men tasted. In addition to the canned food, the *Erebus* and *Terror* carried tea, tobacco, chocolate, rum, and wine.

WARM AND COZY

It is bitterly cold in the Arctic most of the year. Explorers there need winter gear, such as sealskin caps and overcoats. Franklin's ships also used their steam engines to power a central heating system, but the engines used so much coal they did not always run.

My Explorer Journal

★ Imagine you are a sailor traveling with John Franklin. What sorts of things would you bring from home that might be useful?

Found!

Franklin's winter quarters on Beechey Island were found in 1850. The remains of the wooden huts can still be seen today.

KEEP IT CLEAN

+ No bad behavior for crew

Franklin liked to run a clean, **sober** ship. According to letters that were sent home from Greenland, the explorer banned swearing and drunkenness. He thought discipline was important. Every Sunday, Franklin led a church service for his men.

TRAVEL UPDATE

Doomed

★ If you're facing the Arctic winter, follow Franklin's example: make camp. In 1850, searchers found the winter camp Franklin made in 1845 on Beechey Island. The crew had built wooden huts and made tents from **sailcloth**. There was also a carpenter's shop and a kitchen garden, but it was full of moss.

Meeting and Greeting

Not many people live in the harsh Arctic climate. Some, like the Inuit, found ways to survive by ice fishing and hunting animals for food, and using animal skins for clothing.

Did you know?

During his 1854 search for Franklin, John Rae met Inuit hunters who told him about *kabloona*, or white men, who had died west of a large river.

TO THE RESCUE

- ☛ Food for starving Europeans
- ☛ Dene save Franklin's men

Franklin met the Dene, or Copper Indians, on his first trip to the Coppermine River in 1821. The Dene leader Akaitcho helped George Back save Franklin's men at Fort Enterprise. Franklin noted the Dene's "kindness to strangers."

THE PEOPLE

- ★ Surviving the cold
- ★ Explorers have much to learn

The Inuit of northern Canada, Greenland, and Alaska hunted animals such as seals and whales. Inuit hunters made snow shelters named **igloos**. In the summer, families built homes from driftwood and animal skins. Explorers like Franklin learned survival skills from the Inuit.

GATHERING INFO

On Leopold McClintock's 1859 rescue mission, he met an old Inuit man, Oo-na-lee. He told McClintock about a ship crushed by ice off King William Island that had sank in the deep water. The elder then told of another badly damaged ship. He added that his people had found the body of a large man aboard that ship.

Fur

One tip explorers learned from the Inuit was to wear furs to keep warm. Previously, explorers in the Arctic wore only layers of canvas clothes.

HALL HAS HOPE

- Explorer lives among the Inuit

- Hall visits remote island

In 1869, the American Charles Hall visited King William Island. He was fascinated by the Arctic and by Franklin's story. Hall had lived with the Inuit for five years and had heard stories about starving men and their ships. Hall thought some of Franklin's crew must have survived. However, when he finally visited King William Island, Hall found only skeletal remains and other **relics**.

Searching for Franklin

From 1847 to 1859, some thirty search missions attempted to find Franklin. They found little. In 2014, modern methods, along with Inuit stories, unearthed an amazing find.

LONELY GRAVES ON ARCTIC ISLAND

+ Vital evidence found!

In 1850, a search party discovered the graves of three men on Beechey Island. All three had died in 1846. In 1981, scientists studied the bodies. The cold had left the bodies well preserved. The men had suffered from scurvy, pneumonia, and **tuberculosis**. The bodies also revealed high levels of lead, which can cause poisoning.

LOCAL LORE HOLDS CLUES

☛ Inuit hunters pass on stories

In 1848, the Scottish surgeon John Rae was part of a search party organized by Lady Franklin. Rae continued to work as a **surveyor** for the Hudson's Bay Company in the Arctic. He learned much from the Inuit. In 1854, Rae was surveying east of King William Island. He met an Inuk wearing a naval **cap-band**. Rae guessed that the cap-band must have come from a member of Franklin's expedition.

GATHERING CLUES

★ **Rae closes in on Franklin's fate**

★ **Inuit provide clues**

At Repulse Bay in 1854, the Inuit told John Rae more stories. They reported sightings of some forty men dragging boats southward. Rae offered a reward for any artifacts the Inuit had found. The Inuit brought him a sliver plate engraved with Franklin's name and one of Franklin's medals. They also told Rae that the forty men had died near the mouth of the Back River. Rae sent a formal report to the Admiralty to confirm that Franklin had died.

Found!

After 16 years of searching, a Parks Canada underwater team found a sunken ship in the Arctic. On October 1, 2014, the team announced that the ship was HMS *Erebus*.

MESSAGE FROM THE GRAVE

☛ **Historic finding**

☛ **What secrets will ship reveal?**

In 1859, Lady Franklin sent a search party led by William Hobson and Leopold McClintock to King William Island. At Cape Victory, Hobson found a note hidden in a stone **cairn**. The note recorded John Franklin's death in June 1847, and the death of 23 crew members. The note said the survivors planned to walk to Back River. Meanwhile, McClintock found a boat with two skeletons on the island's south shore.

I Love Nature

Ice covers the northern Arctic year round. However, plants survive further south while animals such as seals, polar bears, and whales all live in the snowy landscape.

Hunting

One of the main benefits Europeans hoped to gain from the Arctic was to hunt polar bears and foxes. White fur was a great luxury at home.

LICHEN

★ **Lichen grows without soil**

★ **Tastes great toasted!**

TRAVEL UPDATE

What, no trees?

★ If you're heading into the Arctic, remember that little grows there. Franklin recorded seeing plants with berries and flowers. Farther north, however, the land had only grasses and lichens. Even farther north, where Franklin's men died, there is only snow and ice.

Fungi and algae make up lichen, a type of plant that does not need soil to grow. It grows all over rocks and trees in the Arctic tundra. Arctic animals, such as caribou, feed on lichen, especially during the winter. Franklin and his men ate lichen when they were stranded at Fort Enterprise in 1821. Franklin wrote that it "…was good to eat when moistened and toasted over the fire." It helped the stranded men to survive until help arrived.

NAME THAT BIRD!

+ Officer's journal reveals new species

Two of Franklin's companions on his voyages, John Richardson and Robert Hood, recorded Arctic wildlife in their journals. Hood illustrated the snowshoe hare and moose, as well as unknown species such as the black-billed magpie (right).

BRRRR! SOME LIKE IT COLD

★ **Arctic seas teem with life**

Plant life may be rare in the Arctic, but the sea is full of animals. These animals have layers of **blubber**, or fat, to keep them warm. Polar bears have thick fur. Fish have special proteins to stop their blood from freezing. The Inuit hunted seals, walruses, and beluga whales.

NORTHERN LIGHT SHOW

☞ **Franklin's midshipman makes study**

In Arctic regions, the *aurora borealis*, or northern lights, turn the sky many colors. The phenomenon is caused by charged particles from the Sun colliding with the atmosphere. Robert Hood, who traveled with Franklin to the Coppermine River, first proved that the aurora borealis was an electrical phenomenon.

Fortune Hunting

Much of the Arctic was still uncharted in the 1840s. Britain still wanted a quick route to Asia's riches. They wanted to prosper from the Arctic's minerals and furs, and to make scientific discoveries.

PASSAGE TO THE EAST

☛ **Britain invests to find dangerous rout**

☛ **Failure at every turn**

For over a century, Britain had hoped to gain control of northern Canada and secure a quick route to Asia through the Arctic seas. Although Norwegian Roald Amundsen found the route in 1905, the ice and harsh conditions meant it never became a useful route for Britain.

RUSSIAN RIVALS

+ Britain back in Arctic business

The British Admiralty's interest in the Arctic grew as Russia stepped up its interest. When Franklin proposed his second trip in 1825, he argued that it was important to keep Russia away from the Arctic. The Admiralty agreed and asked Franklin to gather valuable information.

NORTH WES

SHOWIN

CEDED BY RUSSI

WHAT'S THE ATTRACTION?

★ **Which way is north?**

★ **Britain seeks answers**

Franklin's scientific quest was key to his voyages. The British Admiralty asked him to gather information about the magnetic North Pole. In 1845, Franklin carried a dip circle. It measured the angle between the horizon and Earth's magnetic field. By Franklin's voyage, the instrument could also measure magnetic intensity.

Did you know?

Magnetism affects how compasses work. A study of Earth's magnetic field was therefore thought essential to help improve navigation at sea.

ARCTIC RICHES

☛ **Fur trade expands north**

☛ **What lies beneath the snow?**

In Franklin's time, the Hudson's Bay Company, owned by Britain, controlled the fur trade. It had trading posts in the north, where local people hunted arctic fox, lynx, and beaver. The Arctic was also rich in useful minerals, such as zinc and lead. Gold was discovered in the Yukon in 1896.

This Isn't What It Said in the Brochure!

John Franklin knew the Arctic was a dangerous place. He had suffered near-starvation and lost many men. But he did not foresee the disaster of his final voyage.

Did you know?

Years after Franklin went missing, sailors claimed to have seen *Erebus* and *Terror* floating in the ocean, frozen into a large iceberg that was moving in the Arctic currents.

SHIPS CAUGHT IN ICY TRAP

☛ Ice blocks ships

Halted by ice in Lancaster Sound, Franklin and his crew made a winter camp on Beechey Island. Living conditions would have been harsh. Two men died in January and another in April. The survivors were probably weak, but they returned to their ships in the spring and headed south.

MURDER!

★ Young officer shot

★ Voyageur to blame

Robert Hood was a midshipman on Franklin's 1819 expedition. When he grew too weak to go on, Franklin had to leave Hood and other sick men behind. One of them, a **voyageur** named Michel Terohaute, shot and killed Hood. Terohaute was executed for his crime.

WHERE IS JOHN FRANKLIN?

+ Sole clue to Franklin's final days

The piece of paper William Hobson found in the cairn on King William Island is the only clue to Franklin's fate. The paper contains notes written at different times. On May 28, 1847, the note says, "All Well." However, Fitzjames and Crozier added to the note a year later. They confirmed that Franklin had died on June 11, 1847. Many people believe Franklin died onboard the *Erebus*.

POISONED!

★ Mystery still surrounds deaths

In 1981, experts examined the bodies from Beechey Island. They found high levels of lead. They then studied cans of food fom the island. The lead used to seal the cans had contaminated the food. However, most experts think the men did not die from poisoning alone.

DRASTIC MEASURES

☛ Did explorers eat the dead?

In 1854, the Inuit told John Rae they had found bones that showed that some of Franklin's crew had become **cannibals**. In 1997, scientists found knife marks on the bones that proved the story to be true.

End of the Road

John Franklin did not make it through the Northwest Passage. However, his expeditions furthered knowledge about the Arctic and inspired other men to explore further.

A WIFE'S MISSION

- Lady Franklin looks for answers

- Spends her fortune

By 1854, no one had heard from Franklin for nine years. The Admiralty gave up. Lady Franklin did not. She bought a steam yacht, the *Fox*, and hired Leopold McClintock to go to the Arctic. In 1859, McClintock returned to England with the note from the cairn that confirmed Franklin's death.

Heroine

Lady Franklin was widely admired for her search for her husband. A song was written about her. It contained the line "What the nation would not do, a woman did."

FIND FRANKLIN!

★ Admiralty submits to public pressure

★ Searches come up empty

After pressure from Lady Franklin, the Admiralty finally sent three search parties to find Franklin. The Admiralty offered a reward for any news about Franklin's fate. In August 1850, the remains of Franklin's winter camp and the Beechey Island graves were found.

> **"** Of all men he is the best suited for the command of an enterprise requiring sound sense and great perseverance."
>
> *James Fitzjames on Sir John Franklin*

ARCTIC MEMORIES

+ Explorer publishes journals

After Franklin's first expedition to the Coppermine River did not go as planned, he published his journal in 1822, *Narrative of a Journey to the Shores of the Polar Sea*. He published a second journal after his 1825 voyage. Both journals contain valuable information about the geography of the Arctic. They also include illustrations by George Back.

LEGACY OF A LOST HERO

- ☛ **Franklin inspires explorers**
- ☛ **North Pole finally reached**

Franklin's disappearance inspired many explorers to try to find out what had happened to him. They explored more and more of the Arctic. Finally, in 1909, two Americans claimed to have reached the North Pole: Robert Peary (above) and Frederick Cook. The two men argued about who had reached the pole first. Both stories had weaknesses. No one knows for sure the truth about their claims.

PEARY

COOK

"THE ROOSEVELT"

THE BRADLEY

GLOSSARY

blubber The fat of sea animals, such as seals and whales

bomb ships Any type of wooden sailing ships designed to carry a cannon

cairn A mound made by piling up stones, usually to form a landmark or a memorial

cannibals People who eat the flesh of other people

cap-band A band of material that goes around a hat or cap

colony A settlement established by one country in another territory

contamination The pollution or spoiling of something by being mixed with something else

delta A fan shaped area of streams and islands that forms where some rivers meet the sea

empire A number of countries all ruled by the same country

hammocks Beds made out of rope or canvas that are slung between two fixed points

igloos Dome-shaped temporary structures built from snow and ice by Inuit hunters

knighthood A title granted by the British monarch; a knight can call himself "sir"

lead A dull, heavy metal; lead can be poisonous if it enters the human body

lichen A plant that grows like a crust on rocks

looting Stealing something when it is not being looked after

magnetic fields Regions around objects that are affected by the objects' magnetism

midshipman A junior office in the Royal Navy

penal Related to a prison or to punishment

premonition A feeling that something bad is going to happen

propellers Screw-shaped blades that turn to power a ship through the water

provisions A supply of food or other items

relics Objects that survive from an earlier time

sailcloth Canvas or other material used to make sails

scurvy A disease caused by a lack of Vitamin C that results in rotting gums and bleeding wounds

sober Serious and sensible; sober also means not affected by alcohol

surveyor Someone who studies and maps areas of land

tuberculosis A disease that damages the lungs

voyageur A Canadian boatman working for a fur company

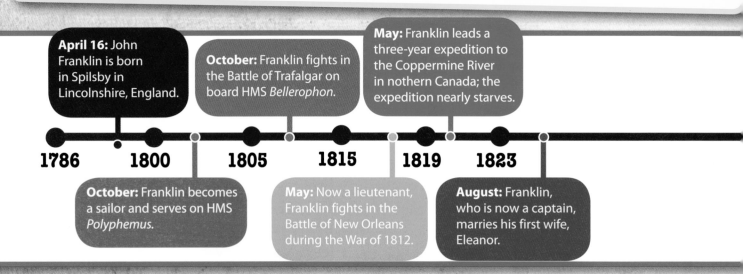

April 16: John Franklin is born in Spilsby in Lincolnshire, England.

October: Franklin fights in the Battle of Trafalgar on board HMS *Bellerophon*.

May: Franklin leads a three-year expedition to the Coppermine River in nothern Canada; the expedition nearly starves.

1786   **1800**   **1805**   **1815**   **1819**   **1823**

October: Franklin becomes a sailor and serves on HMS *Polyphemus*.

May: Now a lieutenant, Franklin fights in the Battle of New Orleans during the War of 1812.

August: Franklin, who is now a captain, marries his first wife, Eleanor.

ON THE WEB

http://teachingkidsnews.com/2014/09/22/2-franklin-expedition/
A report from Teaching Kids News about the discovery of Franklin's ship in 2014.

http://www.enchantedlearning.com/explorers/page/f/franklin.shtml
A biography of Franklin from Enchanted Learning.

http://www.rmg.co.uk/explore/sea-and-ships/facts/explorers-and-leaders/sir-john-franklin-(1786-1847)
Facts about Franklin from Britain's National Maritime Museum.

http://history.howstuffworks.com/polar-history/sir-john-franklin
How Stuff Works biography of Sir John Franklin

BOOKS

Beardsley, Martyn. *Sir John Franklin: The Man Who Ate His Own Boots* (Who was…?) Short Books, 2005.

Foran, Jill. *The Search for the Northwest Passage* (Great Journeys). Wiegl Publishers, 2004.

Hyde, Natalie. *Expedition to the Arctic*. Crabtree Publishing Company, 2014.

Knudsen, Anders. *Sir John Franklin: The Search for the Northwest Passage* (In the Footsteps of Explorers). Crabtree Publishing Company, 2007

Snowden, Maxine. *Polar Explorers for Kids: Historic Expeditions to the Arctic and Antarctica with 21 Activities.* Paw Prints, 2008.

February: Franklin makes a second trip to the Arctic to map the coast of Labrador; Eleanor dies while he is away.

April: Franklin is knighted and becomes Sir John Franklin; Jane becomes Lady Franklin.

June 11: Franklin dies in the Arctic, aged 61; the cause and location of his death are not recorded.

1825 **1828** **1829** **1836** **1845** **1847**

November: Franklin marries his second wife, Jane Griffin.

April: Franklin becomes Lieutenant Governor of Van Dieman's Land (Tasmania), a British penal colony. Many people feel his rule there is too easy for the prisoners.

May: Franklin sets off on HMS *Erebus* on his final expedition to search for the Northwest Passage.

INDEX